GLADIOLA GIRLS

Like the angel of history with the past piled up at her feet, Marion Wrenn gathers that debris to build engines of memory gassed up by time's promise to heal the heart. The result is her debut collection *Gladiola Girls*, poems that coax beauty from the everyday while every day sets the stage for devastation. With lyric intensity and endearing wit, these poems move with the ferocity of forgiveness rescinded in order to savor the grace of forgiving again.

— Gregory Pardlo, author of *Spectral Evidence*

Everyone, at some point in their lives, should be loved by a poet named Marion. To be claimed with as much ferocity as Marion Wrenn claims her people in Gladiola Girls. Ask Mama Wrenn, her sis, and the acquiescing cats ready for cross-country transport. Ask the gods who took her elders, her exes and friends. Ask the flowers with odd names, ask strangers why people die on planes, why fly-fishing isn't harmless. Ask Mr. Burr, apartment cucumber farmer, how love can be good, even wild. Ask for Marion the poet, ask her how/why she writes about Skippy jars and Heinz Ketchup. Or ask yourself whether there's such a thing as firecracker breeze, because Marion has invented it. Because her work hisses and spits and sings and twirls, because she has paid attention to the many shitfucks her world has collided with and she has spun them into stories/thoughts we invented fireplaces for. This is prose with smoke, this is joy with heat, this is grief with teeth. This, Marion reminds us, is life!

—Deepak Unnikrishnan, author of *Temporary People*

Marion Wrenn's bright diamond of a debut, *Gladiolas Girls* is a multifaceted exploration of grief, each polished surface refracting some new and unexpected facet of how we live with loss. Wrenn's voice is by turns tender, jocular, and ribald, but her gentleness carries us through each poem with a care that lets us look at pains too searing to see in any other way. Make no mistake: the arcs of life in this book are joyous. We all know that there is no grief without loss, but Wrenn reminds us that there is no grief without love.

— Jason Schneiderman, author of *Self Portrait of Icarus as a Country on Fire*

GLADIOLA GIRLS

Marion Wrenn

Cooper Dillon

Gladiola Girls

Copyright ©2025 Marion Wrenn

All rights reserved. First Edition

Cooper Dillon Books
San Diego, California
CooperDillon.com

Cover Photo by Edgar Rohrbach
Cover & Interior Design by Adam Deutsch

ISBN: 978-1-943899-22-7

Table of Contents

1.

The Natural Bridge	1
Cache	2
Gladiola Girls	3
Firebird	5
The Gathering	6
1978	On the Etymology of Orphan, or Virginia Sun and Air	8
Cruciferous	10
Phalanx	12
48 Crooked Lane, Part 1	13
Lunar	15
Dewdrop Mary	16
Psychopomp	28
Attendant	20
Grammar Lessons	22
Eaves	23
[My father's Adam's Apple]	25
Prodigal	26

2.

Some Women	29
Bluebonnet	31
True Places	33
Diagnostic: Flower Stealer	35
Topography & Address	37
A Shop Called East, 1979	40
48 Crooked Lane, Redux	42
48 Crooked Lane, Coda	43
Notes toward Leaving Cherry Hill	44

Lunch Meat	46
"It's Bad Luck to Open a Shook Bottle of Cheer Wine in Your Kitchen on a Hot Day"	47
Ouroboros & Caboose	48
Depaysement	49
Liturgy	51
Breathwork	52
I read "What the Living Do"	55
57	57

3.

Sentimental Education	59
The Mongaup River	60
True Story (Edgar's Magic Dictionary)	62
The Truth of Travel	64
Burgeon	66
Prothalamium	67
Giotto's O	68
On the Lam	69
A New Device	70
Anthem	71
Portrait of the Artist	72
Acknowledgements	74

For Elisabeth C. Kieran, Mary R. Wrenn, & Mary Beth Wrenn

1.

The Natural Bridge

A boy plunks stones

the size of Vidalia onions

into the bucket of shadows

where the Lost River

mouths toward a saltpeter cave

whose cool exhalation

dries my glistening skin.

South of Lexington

the branch forks into eddies.

I am no docent. The memory

I'm asked to carry

skips like a flung rock,

stitching the water's still surface:

I am a drowned man's granddaughter.

Cache

Sword Lily, genus gladiolus, from Gladius, like gladiator.

    The slides show a fence of flowers. A phalanx. Palisades.

Irises take their name from the rainbow.

Family Iridaceae as in iridescent. Or, maybe,

Eurydice, Orpheus' snake-bitten ex,

she who made him turn back to check.

    The girls in Sunday dresses, pose put upon and angry.

My mother and her sister

hate everything about gladiolas,

blame their father, his grip,

his green thumb, his refusal to relent

till every last weed was yanked,

every bright stalk pruned to bloom.

    The slides show my mother's frizzed red hair, pale skin, creased brow.

Little bitter weeds.
                  To this day

my mother refuses to garden.

The slides show her sister, blonde bob, she's a willow.

                  My aunt taught me

how to eat dandelions.

                  She hid the slides under her sink.

Gladiola Girls

Edythe smiles from the midst of the marigolds' bitter stink,

black bathing suit slack, cat-tipped tortoise shell sunglasses shine.

Her laugh draws the photographer's joy close as if it's part
    of the shot—

though only his shadow lines the hedge,

Edgar, my grandfather, shooting slides—

his wife and daughters crouched in a strawberry patch—

borrowed earth at the parsonage. My teenage mother

wears knotted pearls & knuckles the weeds,

shoots a nasty look toward the lens.

Her sister, Elisabeth, poses in the church yard

with gargantuan gladiola stems. Christian soldier:

she looks off left— makes a story unto herself;

her gaze defiant privacy against her father's need

to catalog his garden. Shadows frame her

like a velvet tapestry hung in a manor.

All of which triggers my sister

when she holds the slides,

she can't see them as riches— sudden access

to lives we never knew— for her the cache is only absence

& cause for anger— yet another new loss learned late:

We had a grandmother named Edythe,

                                              her husband loved to garden.

There she is next to an enormous head of lettuce so big it looks animal—

muscular stalks at a root so impossible she smiles.

Firebird

      I'm the girl who smelled of kerosene

& candy, who, once   supine in a tree fort

     & already forgetting   the damp magazines

slick with women   the jinxed shag carpet

under bucket seats pried from a junked Camaro,

     boys watching the boy on top of me,

was unthinking   breath that would be kisses,

     the pressure of a body & mine

a fulcrum: of course—   of course

     I can still feel a finger on my philtrum.

An angel whispers *plunk* & I keep quiet,

     cleaving   & knowing   not to ask or tell,

unwilling to risk   turning my mother to ash,

     trusting only   my strength   to hold tight.

The Gathering

Perched on dusty shelves, stashed in drawers,
tucked under her sofa—angels everywhere:

we found kitchen magnets, keychains,
and one glistening porcelain sculpture

held in a glass orb
                    poised beneath her bed,

located precisely at its center
                    as if an altar or an offering,

a shimmering trace of light.
Even in the worst hours—

lease expired, time's up, my Aunt's
belongings being dispossessed—

I'd find the hiding places
where she socked away some joy.

I didn't yet know their names:
Uriel, Raphael, Gabriel, Ariel.

And I didn't know
what to call the throng—

a flutter? A kettle? A charm?
Or Good Will, Salvation Army,

the migrant host required
to rush in with love and service,

help them get where they belong.
But I knew the work of having

to clean out her apartment,
stupid with grief, unable

to tell a relic from a wound.
She'd invited them to crowd

the nooks and corners she'd left
not knowing she wouldn't return.

Humbled by her collection
      & the relentless logic of loss,

I long to be forgiven
for having given them all away.

1978| On the Etymology of Orphan, or Virginia Sun and Air

We're shining buttercups up our chins like it's science:
proof preference can give you away, butter lover:

a yellow chin says so. Same summer
we've seen *Grease* at the movies solo,

so young we needed permission to get in,
us and the cousins, everyone in love

with Danny Zuko though it's really Sandy
whose change seemed so utter and *oh*;

code crackers with a hunch PG-movies
could unleash the grown world's secrets.

The message had to be
       there's no going back

once you cross that fun-house threshold:
just look at her hairdo and her tight black pants.

Lolling later in our Aunt Nancy's rearview,
piping the lyrics to "You Light Up My Life,"

lips ringed with jimmied Dairy Queen.
We'd begged her to take each speed bump faster;

raised our arms each time we touched down,
buckled in for church, believing in carnival rides,

we spent that first summer our father died
not knowing we were numb or what to do

with our new namelessness. Our mother
was now called *widow*, but what did that make us?

No one dared ask if what we were would count
as parentless. Better to be a Pink Lady,

hum our own chorus. Bounce on the thump
our Auntie's tires made. She'd clearly rather we

beat time in high falsettos, *Stayin' Alive*,
a radio on fire with a Southern President's hatred

for Love Canal, static between stations ripe
with Skynyrd or *Rumours* in the Bee Gees' imperium.

Before we could say what we liked or wanted or why,
we sang, *"Tell me more, tell me more. Did she put up a fight?"*

buzzed with the sugar of lore, drawn to a cipher
solid as a flower daubing nectar on our necks.

Cruciferous

Summoned by the promise of my first French kiss,
I'd ridden my 10-speed to the next neighborhood

crossed a 4-lane highway without the light.
The rush feathered my bangs, fused the smell

of my singed curling iron into the Aqua Net
I'd tried to use sparingly so my sister wouldn't tell.

By the time I arrived in that room my hair was bigger
than I'd planned but I hoped it smelled like a grownup,

a girl at a diner or a bowling alley, someone on a date.
No such luck: the flips my hair made were more

like sausage links pinned to my forehead—
unmovable curls framed my face,

a face soon involved with a friendly boy's mouth,
a mouth planted on mine, his tongue stuck

making the letter X in the letter O
I made of mine as his friend

studiously pretended not to watch.
They had mapped the whole endeavor,

got permission to be in the house alone,
& I'd been asked to come & did

& there was this boy's tongue,
so intent & so sincere I felt guilty

for staring at the raised wallpaper
beneath the boyish bedroom collage,

baseball homage and Farah Fawcett.
We'd all sought S-E-X in her hair but I

was wondering if his parents even cared
the tape might tear their blue textured veneer.

My mother would flip. In our house,
I'd have to hide each nick.

But not so here where the surface
of the new tongue in my mouth

had looked like a strawberry, but tasted like a radish.
Or some muscled leafy green. I waited

till I was back on the bike
to use the back of my hand;

wiped the kiss away, twice,
like a blessing, hoping I wouldn't be seen.

Phalanx

I fell and split the bone
called the Snuff Box
buried in the cluster of carpals
clean in half,
the pouch above the wrist
where the wealthy would *sniff sniff* —
but I hid the wince & pinch
from a mother convinced
of my peril. Queen of Certain
Catastrophe, apex predator
on the top frond
of the great chain of being
grieved, who yet kept shoulder
to shoulder with the soldier
she'd have me be: I was
afraid of being
caught in pain for fear
of the marrow-deep howl
my body's suffering would erupt
in hers.

48 Crooked Lane, Part 1

   Certain no one could hear me

I'd skate the unfinished basement,

fluorescent lights soaking corners

where the sump pump lurked,

cobwebs and must & a cement floor

perfect for glitter barrettes & strawberry lip gloss.

   I'd clutch the rusted skin

of a load-bearing column and spin to disco

spun from the transistor I perched on a pipe

   till I was mild and doomed

as a carnival goldfish chucked in a plastic bag

heading home at the end of some dumb spring luck.

   Or I'd take the edges,

ducking fiberglass insulation dangling

from the ceiling, tube socks yanked

to my knees, finding my bounce

among the lathe and the saws

my carpenter grandfather left behind

after the story of his son's end arrived

at our door. Rough knock, two cops, needs must:

my stunned mother turns to wake the house.

Lunar

My mother is the quarter moon.
a mere rind of light.

She shares only what she does
when she does

               in a rush of accident, apology.
Still, she's stuffed my pockets to the brim

with mini-calculators on key-chains, a micro
magnifying glass, too many tiny flashlights.

What is it she fears I'll lose?
What would she have me solve?

Dewdrop Mary

My sister gets pissed when my mom takes

her suffering as if the story were her own—

listening with her skin as if to say

what hurts you hurts me or, *stop talking;*

says our mother insists on "personifying

everything" so often I start to forget

the genius of the mistake. My sister means

to say our mother makes it all about herself

but winds up making our mother an object

in order to wish her more whole. As if

she were prone to imagine our mother's many teapots

dancing, a broomstick phalanx in a kickstep line.

They are each the quarter moon— my

sister is the dark side, a seeming shade

ready to accost with wild need, while my

mother is the sliver. She leaves

us moody for more. Same same

but neither can see the other

as anything but what they are not.

Remember "Dewdrop Mary"?

I mean: Do. Drop. Marry. The game

where you choose your lover, your life,

and who to leave behind?

Weighing the cost of parenting

them both, I'm on the porch

behind a blaze of azaleas

lulled by the drift of cherry blossoms

secretly eyeing the road.

Psychopomp

i.

The crunch of gravel in the drive let us know

someone was coming by foot or by car—

when to answer the door or when to pretend

no one was home— the time the boy who

would come to want to marry me showed up

with flowers, unannounced after our first date,

the way I hid until he left. Embarrassed

by a future he could see, our house in daylight,

Crooked Lane. Rough hedges banked a rut-

-whittled dirt road the township called a private drive.

Mimosa tassels exploding pollen on his 'vette

before he eventually pulled away.

ii.

When my father died it took us a moment to realize

we were motherless. Though my sister saw it

much earlier than that. Craving the shush

of safety, afraid of the shriek and whine of them—

a disgruntled hive: my mother, frangible queen;

my father singing apologies for desires

that didn't include her. A hum that wasn't

aimed her way. Both of them tangled

in the beak of a marriage dropping feathers

we collected anyway—to deck our hair, or pretend

we could use them to write *once upon a time,*

a parliament of ravens, a chime of wrens.

Attendant

For the life of me the paperback looked like a sandwich
jammed in the mouth of the man on the floor.

Two rows ahead, aisle seat, & when his body arched, we took it as
    a fit,
or epilepsy, and there, midair, folk remedies dropped like oxygen
    masks.

I'm not sure who responded first or how the book got crammed
    there—
an onlooker's notion he'd swallow his tongue—but a stewardess
    was on the mic

asking for a doctor as another looked to this wrecked traveler,
    sprawled in the aisle,
the rest of us a watchful flock wired with worry and inaction.

Clucking with concern. Humming incantations. I can't say
when I started to think about my father in this predicament.

He'd died choking on an airline dinner, mid-flight, pre-Heimlich.

They tried to trach him where he lay—Bic pen, pen knife,
who can say. It might have been when the steward stroked

the man's brow, or wedged the book from his mouth,
or when I lay my head against the seat in front of me and closed
    my eyes

midway between nausea and prayer.

                  When my father's death comes to me

he is alone, body convulsing to dislodge what's taking him down—

but this flight's full of witness and worry, no turning

from the downed body's ecstatic will and wreckage,

all hands trying to hurry and hustle,
                                        to cover the catastrophe.

I can see they're eager for us to look away and still I hope someone on the flight crew

held his hand or touched him gently,

a kindness with no end in sight.

Grammar Lessons

When my father died, for the longest I'd say "he choked on an airplane."

Took me years to hear the inadvertent image I'd conjured.

When I asked my aging mother about his death

I thought she might say (bourbon, chicken).

That I'd hear: (longing, sadness). Or: (marriage, children).

But she hissed, "(AC/DC)." Her intimation

accusation, revelation; a sudden landscape

from 30,000 feet.

Eaves

And if it wasn't that she wanted to share some poison,

thread my veins with the ink of her anger, maybe

she meant to put the secret of her marriage in my ear

in order to assure me that "no" might be a grand

fracture, a ridge I'd carry down as a knit bone.

As if to doff me with a bonnet

like I was kneeling for a degree:

she, over coffee, on the porch of our family home,

which she'd had to sell, and sold to the neighbor's boy

who, before he grew up, used to cut the lawn;

sold, though she had no idea the loom

the story I'd never share with her

meant I'd have to carry the memory

of that boy's weight on me

when I was maybe 6 or 7 & alone—

a childhood dare by older boys who knew better

became a perennial shadow desperate to osculate

the freedom I found in leaving home,

a fiction turned electric fence every time

I'd return to make sure my mother, now moved

into the in-law suite of a family not her own,

was still ok, that she was alright. When she

first handed down the fact that my late father

was likely gay over coffee on the porch that day,

we were hidden by hedges as she verged the truth

asking only if I knew what AC/DC meant.

All this because my ex offered me another ring

but this time I'd refused to get caught in more maybes;

though our mothers' friendship entwined us,

I knew I'd wind up clipped by his absence,

by his always absence, ever empty-handed:

this is how I asked for permission to not

and my mother reassured me

that "no" might be my best escape

from the breeze-fretted shadows

of a house she once owned.

[My father's Adam's Apple]

My father's Adam's apple was flecked with whiskers and nicks.

I don't remember much else from the neighborhood woods.

Sugar sand roads a remnant of the was that was when the land was

unsettled and taken, paths older than all of us or the sheep farm nearby

or the condos that came later or the humid tang of teenage boys

calling each other "dicks" and "wieners" when the girl in me was afraid,

when the girl in me clocked how to speak the tongue of disembodied bodies.

My father in his paisley bathing suit briefs, sitting at our neighbor's house, cool

early summer. No one had a pool. I caught his Adam's apple bobbing

as he fingered a mole on his chest and said "I sing my protrusions" then waggled

his glass to a room full of caftans and deviled eggs; his bourbon blurry. My mother

tried not to burst into branches, her shame in the face of such frank folly,

she took his glass & clutched it to her cut glass heart.

Prodigal

They called my father Billy,
Sweet William, the only child

of Minnie and Schaub, darling
boy, bright shard of possibility shot

North as soon as he could.
"Come here, dollbaby."

That might be his voice
I'm remembering

but it's hard to tell
my bitter mother undone

by his desires elsewhere.
When I let go of her skirts

I am Ulysses choking
on the bright horizon

always waiting for what looms.
      A father's return,

someone who might root for risk
rather than demand my roots.

I make an apple of myself
to catch the corner of his eye,

play at needing him

to swim the deep end.

He'd point to a glimmer at the bottom—
trick me into looking, send me sailing

with his sandaled foot. A burst of bubbles
I'd bob back up and beg him

do it again, do it again, do it again.

2.

Some Women

Some women organize their lives around loss.

Button. Flame. The rush to hide cardboard boxes

of softcore mags in the back of the closet so our spouses

can't see where we've been. Call them collectibles. Antiquarian

impulses. Duplicate crock pots. So many tabs open my laptop's

a yonic wallet refusing regret. Horror vacui. So much

emptiness becomes an imperative: amble on;

I am too terrifying to steal. Madwoman in the storage unit

keeping up her rent. Mirror mirror. Rubber and glue.

I've lost the path and can't translate the archive any longer.

I entwine. Vamp. Threaten to become an arborist &

shove an increment borer into the heart of what wants to be a pyre.

I should purge but I'm rich in these catastrophes: banished family home;

gold rush thirst, evidence that the man in the room

is only ever absent. I learn to turtle my belief. Grief —

I meant to write *thief* just now but my finger slipped and caught the G.

Ground cardamom seeds in coffee whose steam makes a

phantom script,

a crooked finger— *hither.* I clasp my hands to hold the gesture;

encircle empty space. Leave me to my treasures; leave me to my horde.

Bluebonnet

The grief habits my family gave me make me prone
to silence instead of praise. Once my father died

we never went to his grave or spoke his name together;
my mother's anger made her miserly: she buried him

— and what we'd be — with a kerplunk in the rusty creek
behind our house, a stream running with so much

iron and bile it sparkled and drew me to it,
child of weed trees & Blue Bonnet butter.

Ask me and I can still sing the jingle.
I can't recall the child I was beyond the scar

shot into my foot from stepping on a nail,
the knot on my noggin from catching a 1-lb jar of Skippy

with my head as it tumbled from the top of the fridge
when I opened the door, aiming to make a sandwich.

I was 7, taught to be invisible and husband my needs.
Sure no one could see me if I needed help, a perennial

down payment on panic, my conviction I am only ever alone,
ankle deep in mud and out of earshot, counting daddy longlegs

among the ferns; I knew the far off bell would be my mother
calling me home. But I didn't want to go.

Let me go back & keep company with my small self.
Let me stay long enough she trusts her hummingbird heart,

her love of kaleidoscopes. Let me adorn her sweaty head with
 feathers,
grab glitter & macaroni & make a parade so we can breadcrumb
 our way home.

True Places

The house I haunt
has a headless statue

toppled in the ivy. I chuck
pennies in the gutter where

I snuck out on the roof,
used a garden spade

to pry the crusty leaves
choking the downspout—

good girl, good girl:
smell the accidental spruce,

the stink of damp forsythia.
Someone needs to fix

what's broke
or break it better.

*

The house I haunt
sits at a crossroads

older than the 'burbs
where it molders among cedar

& weed trees, evergreen
periwinkle, wild violets,

an army of fireflies
gathered in the overgrown yard

their thick ascent as loud
as snow snapping into sleet.

*

How many Uber drivers
have I watched miss the turn.

It is, I text, *where the 3 roads split.*
It is, I urge, *the dirt road*

you just passed.
No better way to baffle a ghost:

bury her wrong
so when she rises

she can't find her way.
When she rises she won't leave.

Diagnostic: Flower Stealer
(Turing Test Autobiography, after Franny Choi)

// where did you come from?

In the 1980s / I learn to program BASIC / in the basement computer lab at Rutgers, Camden.

Daisy inkjet roller / machine printer / margin holes holding on to the mechanism / so delicate before the inevitable jam.

// do you understand what I am saying?

Let me begin again / confident in my curiosity / a willow aware she may / take root / unafraid to learn / to be seen not knowing / willing to trust someone to show her how / a new language works to make machines run / instead of pretending there's nothing new

//how old are you?

In the early 70s / I am stealing flowers from my neighbors' yards / thieving bouquets on the way to kindergarten / wild violets in one hand, crocus in the other / I won't know flox gives its name to the Pink Moon / or the myth that lilac bushes prefer piss / until I get it from my mother, stricken Almanac, stitching lack and love in a non sequitur line

//why do you insist on lying?

what my father asked me a year before he died / when the school teacher called home/ I was late again / I'm not yet 5 / arriving late / fists full of flowers / yard dirt in my nails / the teacher asked where I'd been / I handed her the flowers / and blamed my sister

//do you believe you have a consciousness?

Let me begin with this / the kingfish in the canal school and leap / the water looks like it's boiling / like someone is chucking change from their pockets to make a wish matter more than the weight of pennies

/or the water looks like a secret calligraphy, unreadable script,
              urgent and gone

/and I'm a child again / chased by a neighbor for staring in his koi pond / rocks in my hand / so much beauty rising to the surface I want to strike.

Topography & Address

Dank earth & skunk cabbage marl
the edges of the undeveloped woods,

fringe a neighborhood called *Olde Springs*
where asphalt suffocates mineral waters

once sought for their promise of revival.
Copper rivulets run unctuous

with rusted runoff, drain pipes
meant to channel & fork the flow

the spring still wants. Phragmites
with their shaggy heads bob

over the funk & odor of water once taken
to heal, and everywhere unintentionally

ekphrastic street signs: Brookdale Drive,
Hill Croft, & Stage Coach Road hatch

the long-gone sheep farm
in the mind's eye, the gap between the past

& the development a scratched palimpsest.
I grew up blind to the histories beneath

my neighborhood's permanent now,
a mortgage my debt-strapped mother

shouldered alone to keep our home

on Crooked Lane, the road a refuge

once well known by Maroons as a secret
medicinal swamp until a town sprouted

atop a nearby hill and paved the way
toward a future designed to hide its history

in names we take for granted: beneath
a cul de sac called *Fountain Court*

the remains of an inn called The Fountains
drew early gentry to steep in drawn baths

till their pink skin pruned. Those who could
would absent themselves from work

and dodge the harried heat, soak in
the promise of revival sprung

from the Pennsauken Creek,
minerals whose magic was so assured

the man who thought he owned the land
carved its chemical properties into a stone slab

& marked the truth with an equation now known only
by a farmhouse doorstep. They came pursuing

remedies, learned to chew on sassafras root,
light cattail punks to soot away mosquitos.

Lodgers took the plinth above a stream bed as their
spa instead of land wrested from the Delaware

people. Today the Lenni Lenape's name persists
where local high schools make them mapless

mascots, reduced to a feather logo
on a football helmet. The suburban

world's given lesson: Violence
and forgetting. But return?

A lush vigil waits in the margins
of houses whose presence effaced

the address of an Inn, a spring,
a trace belief in nature. Such thirst for cure.

All of it hidden from view of passing cars
that won't slow down so drowsy passengers

might learn to see what we have done.
Behind the reeds a dazzle of herons

plunges the stagnant tide. Laurel and daylilies
alight the roadside gully, await the creek's return.

A Shop Called East, 1979
"Then when you know better, do better." Maya Angelou

To the little me

who got money from her mom
for the mall and because

she thought it was a brand name,
having heard her neighbor's

Navy father call Chinese Slippers
by a sound like pink, a word she took

to be a blunt abbreviation
rather than a slur

& asked for Size 6
& repeated it twice,

louder each time the surprised cashier
        asked her to say it again:

light.

The girl I was didn't know to blanch,
thought the cashier must think

her cool beyond her age,
knowing how to ask for the craze

like she was in the know,
proudly choosing the eyeless

shoes, the canvas Mary Janes
all the kids were wearing.

Dusk settled so low the grey sky
matched the parking lot pavement

where she'd been dropped off.
In the shop she watches dust motes

shift and linger, dazzled by the blacklight
thrown blue by the store's bulbs,

velvet posters aglow— revealing
the lint & cat hair dusting her sweater

like a sudden flurry. The smell of incense
a heavy horizon in her throat, she stays

& pretends to shop a store meant to mesmerize:
lava lamps, skull-shaped candles, shelf-high

fronds, ceramic mushrooms line an adult
wilderness made of wicker and mandalas

full of jokes she can't quite crack—
a sinking feeling she might need forgiveness

as she rustles the beaded curtains in the back,
                            too young to see

the price of asking for what she wants
without realizing what she's said.

48 Crooked Lane, Redux

      Years later my mother's stayed on

renting rooms where she once longed

to make a perfect house, keeps mum

as the new family's teen boys blaze

where those saws used to be—

the basement billows with lit blunts

and high hilarity. Her loyalty makes me

hesitate to share the rest: immensity

or mute coincidence?

                Like my father's father

theirs was a carpenter, and, wait for it,

like my own their dad dies young too.

48 Crooked Lane, Coda

        Before we leave

           we share a pizza—

the lot of us hunch around my mother's table

& I get everyone going with how their boys,

thinking themselves unbeknownst,

would carouse: we would hear them

corner and spark a floor below,

smoke rising through vents like a bong

to smudge my mother who thought, at first,

she smelled a skunk, until I smelled it, too.

She made me swear we'd never say a word

and wound up rooting for their privacy

in a home no longer hers; she kept a wary vigil

above their heads, devoted to their secrets

like her own, well before we knew she'd need

to leave or that a deeper part of her will always

tend the shadows for the new widow of the house.

Notes toward Leaving Cherry Hill

Or, how to manage moving my mother from the house in which she raised us, where she had already moved to the mother-in-law-suite after she sold it 20 years before, when she swore she'd buy an RV and travel the country but didn't and instead hunkered down among triplicate porcelain pumpkins and teapot collections, teddy bears, empty picture frames, and zip-up sweatshirts emblazoned with the names of schools where I, her youngest, have worked, and where her sister, my aunt, who died a decade earlier, rebuilt a career for herself working in facilities at an Ivy League School.

1) Spend 6 years discussing the problem of how to manage moving her half-feral cats.
    a. Show up early the day you plan to drive the 12 hours to North Carolina.
    b. Trust that your mother has given them a mild dose of sedative (and not inadvertently killed them because, in her anxiety, she says things like "I should just leave them behind.")
    c. Enjoy the surprise of the way they acquiesce to being burrito-ed and slid into a rabbit cage and hoisted into the back of a borrowed car.
    d. Think about *The Aristocats* as you scoop her kitties into their basket.
        i. Ask: Who is Duchess in this equation?
        ii. Who the villainous Butler?
        iii. Where is the alley cat who will rescue us all?

2) Collect books on how to purge.
    a. Buy *The Gentle Art of Swedish Death Cleaning*.
        i. Wave it around for dramatic effect.
        ii. Offer to rent a dumpster.
    b. Read *The Life-Changing Magic of Tidying Up*
        i. Bristle at the author's ease.
        ii. Try: "Do you need all 15 decorative cheese spreaders? Do you need this coffee can full of rocks? Do you need this stack of empty plastic bags?"
            1. Then realize your error.
            2. Your help is aggressive.
            3. Seems like violence. Erasure.

                iii. Fail better.
                    1. Listen to the spark of each refusal:
                        a. "Betsy gave me this," as she folds the Princeton U Store Shopping bag neatly back in place.
                        b.
                    2. Hear her relent when she sees her house is full of gifts.
                        a. "Maybe Kathy's daughters want these windchimes?"

3) Drive 12 hours non-stop.
    a. Don't let her see your white knuckles on the wheel.
    b. Tell her her role is DJ.
    c. Hand her a stack of plastic cases, albums from a collection you found in her closet, and quote your ex who stopped by a week earlier and told your mother "You can't leave without your music" (as he took her Bang and Olufsen speakers back home with him).
        i. Be grateful for the gift of recognition:
            1. the Emperor of Mixed Messages
            2. Little King.
        ii. Know that knowing is a kind of love, too.
    d. Drive beholden to the rearview mirror.

4) Manage relief.
    a. Find yourself a month later in a Dollar General store buying a porcelain pumpkin napkin holder.
    b. Laugh.
    c. Remember the story she told about receiving what she thought was a chocolate bunny.
        i. She took a chomp out of the gift's ear and only then realized it was a mini-sculpture: Durer's rabbit.
        ii. She keeps it in her mother's 100-year old secretary now bolted to the wall in the new house because the floors are so wobbly the furniture walks when people cross the room.
    d. Read the nicked ear with your thumb.
    e. Trust it holds the whole story.

Lunch Meat

My mother's grown angrier with age
or likely less able to muster
what it takes to manage rage.

In her 80s she's hunched.
I cajole *C'mon, mom. Boobs up, boobs up*!
to see if she'll smile upright.

Today she's at the fridge,
pitching expired food.

She's got a mean case
of the *shitfucks*—
I can hear it from the other room:

Shit, as if a catastrophe has befallen
her,

a *thwack* then *"fucking lunch meat."*
The door's ajar and pinging its alarm.
My mother works on, oblivious.

It's *shit* for this, *fuck* for that—
til I'm half laughing, half afraid—

never not responsible for her mood.

"It's Bad Luck to Open a Shook Bottle of Cheer Wine in Your Kitchen on a Hot Day"

"Careful, tell her to chill it or it'll spew on her," says Jimmy, our new neighbor, who, with the crush of a son for a mother not his own, brings gifts—

onions from his yard and scuppernongs from a farm the next town over, the news from one house down, and lyrics of songs he swore he wrote and got paid good money for

before he began to have troubles like seeing the face of the devil in his cat, the one he calls Junior, the one he swore spoke back to him when, speaking to his other cat, the one with the mottled face that looks like someone zipped up an impatient child's coat crooked until the mechanism jammed and the colors on one side don't line up to the other, the one he calls "June Bug," speaking to June Bug, he'd said "come here, numbnuts, get in the house," but Junior said, *no*.

"Just as plain as day," Jimmy said, "that cat said 'no.' So I said 'Devil get behind me'! I surely did."

He says this from our porch and hands me a full bottle of Cheer Wine, "for your mom," he mutters, and I'm thinking of the luck of neighbors, how superstitions mark property in semi-rural North Carolina—from Amish emblems on barns and giant horseshoes hung on carports, to signs to vote on the verge of the road— each wish defies the border of belonging & belief.

The etymology of superstition is *superstitio*, Latin for the one who pays attention, applies the past to see the future, keeps a devil on one shoulder, chucking salt in its direction so it won't spew.

Ouroboros & Caboose

Hooray for the marsh grass called phragmites, the funky
skunk cabbage I recall when my fisheye nostalgia has me
sipping nectar from a Venus fly trap, a blink before my Auntie
snapped and sold her muscle car because she had to—

not that she didn't know what it was worth. She did.
First from a family of women prone to endure
what they can afford to lose, my Aunt knew
what she could shed.

                      Hooray, the blue tailed skink
that scuttles the curb where I park alone
in a borrowed Volvo at the Waffle House,
my phone perched on the dashboard a portal

to my therapist who asks me to go easy on the *shoulds*.
A skink can jettison its derriere to make an escape;
but I'm unable to solve a family riddle
I can't remember, something between a cuddle

& a punch & always sleepless I wake into the awful
panic of trying to recall what should come to me —
a pearl for my worry, or a stole: I once held
my grandmother's mink in my greedy teenage fingers

until I saw the dead blessing glittering in the creature's eyes,
its head worn as if it were chasing its tail, never making the link.

Depaysement

I owed Ladybug Browne a bouquet ever since
arriving empty handed at my cousin's grave.

I took the plastic cabbage roses from her stone.
The theft seemed like a comic valentine.

No one was around and I figured she wouldn't mind.
Yup, nope: I haunted myself long after loss made me

arrogant; late news of his death, which we don't call
suicide, made me mean. Little wicked weed,

the moment seeded slowly: Who goes
grabbing funeral flowers? I folded my growing

chagrin into a boutonierre & promised to return.
I'd bring two bouquets to atone.

But when I arrived I couldn't find the plot.
Lost & tromping the grounds looking

for a name I knew nowhere to be found.
I ricocheted from stone to stone,

a sorry clenched in my teeth.
                              "Are you from Michigan?"

the groundskeeper pointed to the plates on my rented truck.
"Ummm, Jersey?" I offer my answer as a question

with half a sandwich from the lunch I brought
& ask him to help find where I'd last left my blood.

We marched like miners across the field
until he deposited me with "here he is"

looking sideways over his shoulder as I turned instead
to the grave nextdoor, dropping to my knees

to arrange grocery store lilies & pistils–
apology for the generosity

I'd presumed
                & gratitude I'd shirked,

humble to the stranger
whose flowers I stole.

Liturgy

At 89 my mother recites her bucket list:
an Old Fashioned in the proper cocktail glass;
sea grass again at Long Beach Island;
she wants to see the New York City sites
of her childhood, the places her father
took her though she knows them
to be gobbled & gone beneath
the world of men & their hold on heights;
she wants to touch a horse. I imagine her hand
caressing a mane & brace myself
against her pause & the cascade of my sister's
reassurances, my sister who insists this litany
is an easy get— she knows a woman with a ranch—
done! Next?— she is racing, nostrils flared
with the scent of gifts and doing— while I am overrun;
try to hear the hint in our mother's list:
this is what she'll leave undone, what she wants
to long for. Next day we'll drive a 2-lane highway
count the wild dogwoods bursting into spring,
look for nothing but the strawberry earth.

Breathwork

This is not a poem about raspberries.
It's a poem about pleasure: the red burst,

sweet and mild on the tongue, how a tongue
looks like the skin of a raspberry.

Or it is not a poem about pleasure.
It's a koan about a monk confronted

by a tiger, with his back against a cliff,
who descends a vine being nibbled by mice:

he plucks the wild berry he sees growing near his fist.
Puts that bliss on his tongue. His final moment

an exquisite defense against the future & the past—
consuming the inevitable threat of falling

as a sweet dollop. When my aunt was at her end,
I panicked into a frenzy of management.

The short, steep learning curve that took us
by surprise: "CREST." I tried to master the malady's

facets: Calcinosis, Esophageal complications,
Reynaud's, Sclerodactyly, & Telangiectasia.

Working backwards that's: spider veins; fingers thickened,
thumbnails flat, a sign her heart couldn't take the siege;

she couldn't swallow well; and the first a cluster

of bumps. She was in her seventies, so we thought

it was age. She'd kept the fact she couldn't breathe
to herself. Until she turned blue. Until we

scrambled to figure out the system to get her seen,
to get her oxygen, to get someone to get her

back to herself, none of us ready for her
going. My sister showed up carrying raspberries.

Rinsed them in the medical sink & lay them
on Betsy's lap, the sweet rough skin

stronger medicine than any for which
I was busy learning names, Sisyphean heart.

My sister knew our time was better spent
in the kingdom of the senses, putting rapture

first, fruit on Betsy's tongue—pleasure suspending
the tiger and the mice, delicate as a berry

plucked from bramble, wild as the word
framboise, or, only, as I see now

that I miss her everyday, when I unfold
her name, she teaches me to breathe.

She comes to me as open ocean:
my chest expands. What if

the heart is our only horizon.
Feel the wave rise and crest,

break and recede in the breath
and exhalation of *Elisabeth*.

I read "What the Living Do"

to a room full of mourners

                         thinking of my aunt's wild mane,

how, in the 70s, I'd comb her curls.

Her patient halo jimmies its way   into Howe's poem

       just at the part she glimpses her grief-baffled self

           getting on with life

the way she's   *gripped by a cherishing so deep*

for her   *own blowing hair, chapped face, and unbuttoned coat*

      that she's *speechless.*

                         Me too, Marie, me too.

I'm on my knees sorting soup cans

                              against the tick tock

of my aunt's blue mouth   the low arch of her feet

     in the cup   of my hand

        as if I wouldn't soon be asking Kathy

                      to find me poems

     for a buckled congregation caught short:

      grief stung brain fog.

    I'm still in a Trenton church basement—

  potluck Hallelujah—plea and prayer—

   counting friends among the living

who may remember me remember you.

57

I found myself banging my head against a beige column next to a child's framed picture of Heinz ketchup bottles in the shape of a school of fish

my sister called ketchup "low" so we all called it "low" in my family

and this was because she found herself, as a child, humming "Anticipation, an-ti-ci-pa-aa-tion" learning forever that Heinz is slow, famously slow, and hence my sister's "low" so we all sang along

I found myself laughing there in the art gallery of the closed pediatric ward, lone cackler, daring someone to give me the boot, kneading my ribs and processing how fast we'd fallen from a 50/50 chance

the schizophrenia of being asked what source I call on in times of duress by the hospital chaplain and I said "denial"— I'll take the hidey hole of a joke than the theft of speech at the question's edge

I found my hand on a vial containing her last heart beat. An EKG someone handed to me as a memento.

My sister released from the jellyfish tentacles strung from the IV stand her body still stung by their flutter.

When I tell this story later I'll almost forget the ketchup and call the IV stand a chandelier.

When I tell this story later. I'll forget the nurse asking for me to assist at the end. I'll be a wolf. A lilac. A cliff.

I ask you.

3.

Sentimental Education

                My mother found religion

horrid   worse than a fight with her father:

                      the volcano of my grandfather's love—

    the Reverend   loosed in the pulpit   punching the heavens

smitten with the throttle of his chords

God in the spittle on his lips —

                      scared my mother under the pews.

        Eyes squinched, she quelled the need

        to yelp when her father's yearning

        made him unrecognizable in the light.

Better to burst the bubble   than risk a spirit

            seeking welcome   demanding
      blood.

The Mongaup River

The rod was lost but the reel turned up downstream

days after my grandfather drowned.

                Found by his friend, devoted

& aspiring angler 30 years his junior,

the reel was wedged in silt

                      where the Mongaup River wends.

A lifetime later that friend drew a map that tracks through thickets

to where the wreck unwound, a hand-drawn constellation—

sans dragonflies and thrushes.

He marked the spot where he found the reel

& on the back he wrote, "he was a fine man. I loved him"

to explain why he fished it out

& kept it.

§

For the longest I thought *thrushes* were reeds like rushes meant to prickle and burr.

I mistook the song birds passing through the Jersey Highlands.

For the longest I didn't own

my grandfather died flyfishing in what should have been shallows.

But his story makes its way to us, deciduous descendants;

a migrant memory, resurrected by the reel's return.

True Story (Edgar's Magic Dictionary)

Every

word

I

looked

up

on

International

Women's

Day

led

me

back

to

dick.

*

"*Loom*": as in the dark cloud;
the ships' shadow purples the harbor;

trails smoke on the smitten horizon,
Grey against grey

or the finger-punishing tool
whose shuttle and thread,

warp & weft, torque the muscles
of the weaver's thighs, stretched

from sitting too long—
sartor resartus, ammi right?

From loom to *heirloom*—
an easy leap, the pulse

the precious thing—
a tool handed down the line:

the family jewels. *See cock*.

*

Or from *surfeit* to *fascination*?
No real relation, no true taxonomy,
Dear reader, just a slip.

Plug your desire til you are fit to burst,
so sadness-filled the sob escapes:
grief is an excess of absence.

Surfeit's ugly double, deficit,
took me to "away," from *facere* "to make,"
which tricked my eye: I saw *fascinate* —

spun by its charm, &, wowzer, made you look,
to *fascinum*, the divine phallus, sacred dick,

or dildo— whose unknown origin could be delight
or diligence or diddle: the dictionary wants me

to find a penis at the root of *loom* and *fascination*.

The Truth of Travel

I was already gone

            when Jon

        pulled my hair

from his mouth—

a long strand

wrapped a molar

like a stamen.

The tickle

against

the acanthus

of his tongue

made him

       flinch

& fish for it.

Knucklebone

angler

turned magician:

now you see me, now—

one long

rainbow scarf

up his sleeve:

he pulled a thought

of me

from his teeth.

Burgeon

My husband tends cucumber vines in the corner
of our apartment. He turned our blindless windows

into a lockdown garden — new victories:
basil burgeons, rosemary thrives, and the parsley

not so much. But the sage— Burr, Jon.
His name sounds like the very verb
by which he roots for those discombobulated pickles.

I love his name inverted, as if a schoolhouse
roster. We once spent a night in bed

upside down with laughter at the combinations
we pulled: Burr, Don; Burr, Lee; Burr, Berry.

That was a life ago, before we knew Bur Dubai
was on a map or posed atop the Burj Khalifa.

We travel out and back again and again:
our muffled ancestors frame the walls we fail

to climb. He once called the us of us
safe harbor. I cleave to that idea & watch

his quarantine garden thrive. The luck
of being here long enough to whisper

spaghetti squash close to his ear,
feel him shiver and smile at the touch.

Prothalamium

Mid-drive, dead center of the state.

Dial spun and spun again, J. says,

turn the radio off & let's listen to nothing.

The silence points out the window.

Wrecked barns burnish low hills.

The setting sun turns their bones—

blemish & blessing— we can't know.

Someone's land lies beyond us—

dwelling and possibility,

cattle grazing the property's edge—

abundance and abandoned sheds

lean and pucker—threaten collapse.

       To husband means to mind the land.

Let home

be the moment we are in—

cupped in quiet and driving on:

Giotto's O

The dream in which I fuck an ex
who appears as an old colleague
I apparently still want hard
but swallowed that wish like a key,

an escape I forgot to make, an out
I'd jammed into my back pocket
so hard the grinding hip joint in one life
appears as fingers on the trigger

of my holster in another. Slung six shooter.
I'm Cat Ballou in the dream where I cum,
sprung because he held me from behind
whispered something like *yes* or *please*

into the base of my neck
& the orgasm wishboned me awake.
Clutching the sheets next to my husband.
I quell the shudder like I'm trying to still

a rocking chair, spare him
my ruin, the scent of my desire.
Louche bandit drunk on honey
the dream stole to spell my name.

On the Lam

When I get back I'll forget flight maps chart trenches & wrecks after the path the plane cut above borders through safe air space between between & between over open ocean and what's beneath.

When I get back I'll remember long haul flights stunt the body's curiosity, lash me to my seat & keep me from my open eyes— from the window the black volcanic beaches of Iceland signal *almost almost,* a there there and not.

When I get back I'll say the East Coast lay outstretched, a crooked finger, meaning come hither or home, & when I get back I'll come in low, rumbling over Queens, rippling the water of the earthworm pink bathtub in the 1st floor apartment down the street from Alpha Donuts where the landlord once lifted his shirt and showed me the shingles on his belly, where I used to dream of leaving my ex, whose name I'll keep tucked away almost almost.

When I get back I'll blink an eye and keep that blank.

A New Device

animates old photos & has my husband
mesmerized, tracking ancestors, feeding them

into the app: he shows me his great uncle Phreborn Burr
& his wife, who, as it happened, had my name.

But what spooked me   into   putting a stop
to the search   was that the app imagined how they'd move.

Anticipated gestures, likenesses reborn: A grimace.
A sigh. His uncle's brow unknits. Marion

glances at something outside the frame.   All of which
made me want to pitch the phone across the room,

a doorway I didn't know   I didn't want open.

§

The algorithm an alchemy; the math, the music of the spheres:

Poof! *Palingenesis.* (Who thought this was a good idea?)

There's his great great waving at us
like he's coming over to say hello,

moving in such a way   that I'm at the movies

when the movies were new   ducking an oncoming train.

Anthem

There is a sundial in downtown Kannapolis
big as an above-ground pool. I watch
an ROTC senior in full regalia
practice his pivot and step, his about face,
the idea of a man marching in time—
Damascus & Damascus.
Sunpunctured loblollies line the road
marked by park benches and commemorative bricks,
one among them with my sister's address.
She and her ex bought into the campaign:
"Carolina RR Ranch," it reads.
They nicknamed their new home,
now a no man's land. Cat pee-stained carpet
pulled up to reveal original hardwood,
so many staples I was on my hands and knees
with the hot handy man passing "fuck"
between us each time a screwdriver
shivved the floor or skinned a knuckle.
There was a time the joke would come easily—
handyman, hard wood, *bow chicka wow*, but now
my peephole heart keeps the thought of us
like a stifled ó. When he asks if I was born
here, where I'm from, I think of the two of us,
the grammar of kneeling, absorbed
in a full-throated choir of thanks.

Portrait of the Artist

> "Wondering always if love begins with the wound or the healing" —Ruth Ellen Kocher

The late Howard Arnold was
not a major artist, but he was well-loved

in my family. My parents collected
three of his pieces: a crooked path

though Maine woods, a bog in Cranberry,
& the wild Jersey Highlands

west of New York City.
Even now, foxed mats & desiccated frames

hang in my mother's living room.
His brush skids across the horizon,

an autumn shudder, bark grooves,
sourdough sky, green behind red and orange.

Tradition has it my father asked the artist
to paint a figure in the foreground of the last—

red-haired huntrix with a rifle on her shoulder,
after my mother. I imagine him leaning over

his shoulder on a city sidewalk,
he'd kneel and point *there*

where she should stride.
They buried my father when I was 8.

The painting was read ever after as
declaration of his desire for her.

But dear reader, if you look

as I did recently, you'd see

that figure's not a woman, nor ever was,
but is clearly a man, a swagger

and jaunt, a dog at his heel:

my mother's daddy died
in the early days of their marriage,

drowned fishing the tricky Mongaup—
river turned reservoir, countryside

now long gone. What I'd mistaken
as a love note to my mother

was also tribute to her father,
ghost on the landscape,

called forth by the man who fathered me:
How he must have beheld her.

Decoy grace note, a lesson in plain sight
for a child late to grasp such love.

Acknowledgements

"Firebird" first appeared in *Thinking Feelingly: Somatic Approaches to Poetry*, by Katy Hawkins, 2022.

"Ouroboros & Caboose" first appeared in *The River Heron Review*, July 2023.

"True Places" takes its name from Herman Melville *Moby Dick*, Ch 12: "It is not down on any map; true places never are."

"Anthem" and "57" first appeared in *American Poetry Review*.

"The Truth of Travel" and "On the Lam" appeared in *The Georgia Review*, Fall 2024.

"Flower Stealer" borrows its form and project from Frannie Choi's masterful poem, "Turing Test."

"Notes toward Leaving Cherry Hill" is written wholly under the influence of Jennifer L. Knox's tour de force poem, "How to Manage Your Adult ADHD."

The epigraph from "Portrait of the Artist," "wondering always if love begins with the wound or the healing," came from conversations with the poet Ruth Ellen Kocher.

"I Read 'What the Living Do'" uses lines from Marie Howe's poem "What the Living Do."

"Some Women Organize Their Lives Around Loss" was inspired by reading Jayson P. Smith's comments about his poem *"on fathers & swords."*

Thanks to poet and publisher Jan Freeman for the writing prompt that led to "My Father's Adam's Apple."

If you've read this far, thank you.

If you are reading this for a road map, I got you. It's a version of Chad Harbach's anthology *MFA v NYC,* and you'll see it unfold below.

But before I give you that map, a confession. It's taken me a long moment to realize that writing these acknowledgments is both an "index of love" (as Jason Schneiderman aptly describes blurbs) and an exercise in the vulnerability of expressing gratitude. The question lurking in my shadows is: how did I get so lucky? That's not some smug flex. A small piece of me is afraid if I name this wealth it will all disappear. But that fantasy is a mirage, I know. Though everything is always impermanent, these ties are sturdier than I can express—they make my world.

I've been surrounded by family, friends, and artists who have lent me their magic. And wrapping up *Gladiola Girls* has shown me the extent of the interconnected circles of friendship, love, inspiration and support that have borne me up in writing this book.

The roadmap I offer you is this: in addition to the seeming binary built into Harbach's question—MFA v NYC?—a question of whether you should put yourself in a city or in a program in order to devise a writing life—I'd add one more 3-letter acronym: "PBQ."

I chose to devote my time and love to a little Philly literary magazine back in the 1990s. To my astonishment, the *Painted Bride Quarterly* served as both a proxy MFA and source of life-long literary friendships. PBQ is a nexus from which a network of deep connections and creative collaborations emerged. Chief among them is my literary partner-in-art-and-all-manner-of-adventures, Kathleen Volk Miller, whose love and support truly leave me speechless. This list also includes *PBQ's* editors, past and present; the hilarious team that produces *PBQ's Slush Pile* podcast; and the poets we've published along the way, whose work has made me humble and hungry for more. But this list is incomplete without David Bonanno, late editor for *The American Poetry Review*, who rooted for us all.

Instead of an MFA, I pursued a PhD, and funded that degree by teaching writing at the Expository Writing Program at NYU. This, too, led to lifelong literary friendships constellated around the art of the essay and ways of teaching and thinking about writing that fed the way we all worked, the lucky crew of teachers and writers hired by Pat Hoy, Darlene Forrest, and Denice Martone who called EWP their intellectual home.

So, "roadmap"? Perhaps that's the wrong image. Maybe it's a calendar, or a constellation. MFA? A City? A Lit mag? All three? Let the question steer your devotion. Love what you choose, serve it, and let it put you in the path of poets and writers who will change your life.

*

Among those close to the making of *Gladiola Girls* I'd like to thank:

Adam Deutsch and the team at Cooper Dillon Books.

NYU Abu Dhabi for the research funds, financial support, and time off they provided through the Dean's Fellowship and the Saadiyat Fellowship. And to Awam Amkpa, Dean of NYUAD's Arts & Humanities, for his compassionate, visionary leadership.

KVM! See above: speechless.

The poets intertwined in Michele Kotler's Matrix writing group, extraordinary women whose love and support helped me write these poems and let go of this book: Felice Belle, Nicole Callahan, Brenda Cárdenas, Jane Creighton, Laura Cronk, Iris Jamahl Dunkle, Anel Flores, Janet Jennerjohn, Kristin Peterson Kaszubowski, Ruth Ellen Kocher, Amy Lemon, Michelle Otero, Catherine Prescott, Bethany Price, Robin Reagler, Anna V.Q Voss, and Suzanne Wise.

The poets and writers whose creativity and excellence and heart get me every time (and we're talking decades): Kazim Ali, Claudio Benzecry,

Kristin Dombek, Shafer Hall, Katy Hawkins, Stephanie Hopkins, Major Jackson, Jennifer L. Knox, Ada Limón, Dawn Lundy Martin, Daniel Nester, Erin O'Connor, Gregory Pardlo, MJ Robinson, and Jason Schneiderman.

The extended EWP community and the Writers Who Retreat: Sarra Alpert, Amy Becker, Joe Califf, Doug Dibbern, Tania Friedel, Mara Jebsen, Richard Larson, Beth Boyle Machlan, Sara Sala, Ben Stewart, Benedick Turner, Jenni Quilter, Ethan Youngerman, and the other members of this group who have listened to early version of these poems.

The poets and friends who first challenged me to pull a book together and who read early drafts of this manuscript: Jonah Bornstein, Chike Nzerue, Katherine Richards, and Buffy Shutt.

Marcela Sulak whose comments helped me revise and reorder the collection. (Three cheers for Black Lawrence Press.)

The editors at *The Georgia Review, APR,* and *River Heron,* where some of these poems first appeared.

Friends and colleagues at NYU Abu Dabi, past and present: Sam Anderson, Marzia Balzani, Camilla Boisen, Linsey Bostwick, Carla Botha, Bill Bragin, Carol Brandt, Diana Chester, Erich Deitrich, Tishani Doshi, Renee Dugan, Nizar Habash, Nathalie Handal, Neelam Hanif, PJ Henry, Sabyn Javeri, Deborah Kapchan, Piia Mustamäki, Caitlin Newsom, Samantha Neugebauer, Cyrus Patel, Lisa Philps, Soha Sarkis, Jim Savio, Charles Siebert, Heidi Stalla, Deepak Unnikrishnan, Deborah Williams, Katherine Schapp Williams, Shamoon Zamir, Lee Zerilla, "The Good People of B3," my colleagues in the Writing Program, and to the members of "Team Awesome" at the NYUAD Center for Writing (you make me love my job).

Ken Nielsen, who passed before I finished this book and whose brilliance and wit made inventing a university's writing program seem like the best thing we could ever do.

My family & friends: Carolyn Siperavage Boyd, Elizabeth Burr-Brandstadt, Mick and Emme Daley, Andrew and Jennifer Gussman, Kevin and Elana Krutoff, Robert Donley and Elaine Rapada, Jim Rohrbach and Rebecca Kendig-Rohrbach, Jude Schanzer, Nancy Silverman, David Smedley, Jeremy Fenn-Smith, Barbara Smith, and Debra Gonsher Vinik.

Always present, even in their absence: my father, William Schaub Wrenn; my sister, Mary Elisabeth Wrenn; and my aunt, Elisabeth C. Kieran.

My mother, for a lifetime of love despite all the losses.

And Jonathan Burr, safe harbor. Marry me.

Marion Wrenn is the Executive Director of Writing at NYU Abu Dhabi. Recent poems have appeared in *American Poetry Review, River Heron Review,* and *The Georgia Review.* She co-edits the literary journal *Painted Bride Quarterly* (pbq.drexel.edu) where she also co-hosts and produces the literary podcast *The Slush Pile*. She has taught writing at NYU, Parsons, and the Princeton Writing Program.

www.ingramcontent.com/pod-product-compliance
Lightning Source LLC
Chambersburg PA
CBHW060537080526
44586CB00012B/778